SOME
Bible Questions &
Answers

For Those Who Want
To Keep It Simple

Karl W Law

"My people are destroyed for lack of knowledge…"
Hosea 4:6

Cover photography used by permission:
Tyssul Patel
hello@tyssul.co

Published by:
Dr. De'Andrea Matthews, Founder and CEO
Claire Aldin Publications, LLC
www.clairealdin.com
(A faith-based company whose foundation is the Lord Jesus Christ.)

All scripture quotations are from the Holy Bible, King James Version, in the public domain.

Printed in the United States of America.

International Standard Book Number: 978-0-578-68385-0

Library of Congress Control Number: 2020907776

Memorial

In memory of my brother Ethan Pitts who passed before we had opportunity to really get to know each other as brothers.
April 17, 1961 – May 27, 2020

In memory of my cousin Sean Law who fell victim to the pandemic of the year 2020.
November 30, 1967 – May 1, 2020

Jas 4:13-15 "Go to now, ye that say, Today or tomorrow we will go into such a city, and continue there a year, and buy and sell, and get gain: Whereas ye know not what shall be on the morrow. For what is your life? It is even a vapour, that appeareth for a little time, and then vanisheth away. For that ye ought to say, If the Lord will, we shall live, and do this, or that."

"Over the years I have read a lot of books about God, Christianity, and salvation, but this book takes complex questions and simplifies them in a way that everyone can understand. This would make a great text for catechism study."

~Tyisha Hurst
Minister
International Miracle Gospel Tabernacle Church

"I am thoroughly impressed at the labor obviously rendered in this writing. This book will be a blessing to the believer, as well as an answer to the curiosity of the non-believer. This literary tool is an asset to the Body of Christ and should be utilized in the furtherance of Christian education. Well done sir!"

~Jason Smith
Pastor
Bethlehem Judah Church

"This book is a great introduction to the wisdom, knowledge, and understanding God desires for His people. It breaks down the foundational and life changing themes of the Bible for everyone to understand. This is a good body of work for the Lord!"

~Kelley Gupton
Minister
International Miracle Gospel Tabernacle Church

"How often it has been said, 'the most profound things in life come to us in the simplest of manners.' *SOME Bible Questions & Answers* is an easy guide for any follower of Christ, but especially for those seeking the answers to life's questions of the heart about God's Word. This book will serve as a great reference for any seeking to know the everlasting way."

~Terry Robinson
City Director
Campus Crusade for Christ

Dedication

This work is dedicated to:

- God the Father – The Creator of Heaven and Earth.
- Jesus Christ the Son – The Saviour of the world.
- The Holy Spirit – The One Who guides into all truth.
- Earl Doram and Mary Pitts, my biological parents, without whom I would not be in this world.
- Charles and Ethel Law, my adoptive parents, without whom only God knows where I would be today.
- Charnelle, my beautiful and lovely wife, a blessing from the Lord.
- Karlie and K'Mari, our daughters, children of my latter years, extensions of God's grace and mercy to me.
- Robert Eddie, the Brother in Christ who took the time to share the Good News with me so that I could partake of The Tree of Life in 1984 on the campus of The University of Michigan. I am praying that the Lord will cause our paths to cross once again on this side.

- The late Pastor Dr. Frederick G. Sampson and Tabernacle Missionary Baptist Church.

- Pastor Kenneth Hampton, Sr. and Grace Bible Chapel Church.

- The late Pastor Bugsby, Pastor Doug Sarver, and Warrendale United Brethren in Christ Church.

- The late Pastor Bennie Harris, Jr., Mother Lorraine Harris, Pastor Bennie Harris, III, Sister Serena Harris, and The Prayer House Church.

- Pastor Charlie Gupton, Jr., Sister Yvonne Gupton, and International Miracle Gospel Tabernacle Church.

- My immediate and extended family.

THANKS TO ALL WHO HAVE HELPED THE VISION
BECOME A REALITY!

Table of Contents

Introduction

This work is an outflow of a series of Sunday School and Bible Study classes that the Lord has allowed me to stand in the place as teacher to conduct. Nowhere is it implied or expressed the answers given are exhaustive, but they are what the Holy Spirit gave me at the time of formation. The answers also represent the gleanings of wisdom from others that I have had the privilege and honor to sit under – some of which are mentioned in my Dedication.

As the title states – these are *some* Bible questions & answers for those that are looking for concise and simple responses for one's own knowledge and/or to share with others. One may say that God is deep so how can you simplify it? Yes, God is deep, but "we" do not have to be to the point where we confuse people when a simple question is asked. "God is not the author of confusion" (1 Cor 14:33). He designed His Word so that even a child can know who He is. When a believer is sharing the Word of God with an unbeliever, the believer must be mindful of the fact that he or she is not the only one talking. The enemy is also talking. Therefore, the believer must be able to give his or her response simply, quickly, and straight to the point. Too much and the person's attention is lost. Some plant, some water, but God gives the increase (1 Cor 3:6). The believer ought not to think that he or she must get it all in in one meeting. Prayerfully the Lord will open the door for further engagement, but the believer's goal should always be to SPEAK LIFE because souls are at stake and time is of the essence.

This work is also intended to debunk some of the traditions that have been passed down through the years within the church, traditions pertaining to the Word of God that have caused the people of God to believe lies instead of knowing truth. "My people are destroyed for lack of knowledge" (Hosea 4:6). The people of God are powerless if they don't know the truth of the Word of God (John 17:17). The enemy attempted to misuse the Word of God against Jesus, but since Jesus IS the Word of God the attempt failed. It is of utmost importance that in this day and time the people of God know the Word of God so the enemy can't misuse the Word of God against them – any attempt in like manner, as with Jesus, will fail.

The Lord God is not giving any new revelations because He has said all and given all in His Word. As we grow closer to

Him, as we "grow in grace and in the knowledge of our Lord and Saviour Jesus Christ" (2 Pet 3:18), He opens our eyes and our understanding to that which He has already revealed. It is my prayer that this small work will be a blessing to all who read in that endeavor. Thank you for your prayers and support.

~Karl

Preface

My Heart Goes Out to the unbelieving, the lost, the broken hearted, the wayward, the hopeless, the seeker, the disenchanted, the cynic:

I speak a Word of Life to you – Jesus loves you and He has a unique plan for your life. A part of that plan is to fill the void which is in every man. This void can only be filled by the Spirit of the Lord Who is God. Man tries all that he can to fill the void with things of the world, traditions and doctrines of men, but whatever is put in that place will never be fulfilling. There may be a temporary satisfaction, but eventually it will turn dry. I encourage you to allow the Lord Who is God to fill the void that is in you through His Son the Lord Jesus Christ.

Psalm 118:8 *"It is better to trust in the Lord than to put confidence in man."*

To the believer:

"The devil tempts us to destroy our faith, but God tests us to develop our faith because a faith that can't be tested can't be trusted. False faith withers in times of trial, but True Faith takes deeper root, grows, and brings glory to God."

~Wiersbe, The Bible Exposition Commentary

Bible Book Abbreviations

<u>Old Testament</u>

Gen – Genesis

Ex – Exodus

Lev – Leviticus

Num – Numbers

Deut – Deuteronomy

Josh – Joshua

Judg – Judges

Ruth – Ruth

1 Sam – I Samuel

2 Sam – II Samuel

1 Ki – I Kings

2 Ki – II Kings

1 Chr – I Chronicles

2 Chr – II Chronicles

Ezra – Ezra

Neh – Nehemiah

Esth – Esther

Job – Job

Ps – Psalms

Prov – Proverbs

Eccl - Ecclesiastes

S of S – Song of Solomon

Is - Isaiah

Jer - Jeremiah

Lam - Lamentations

Ezek - Ezekiel

Dan - Daniel

Hosea - Hosea

Joel - Joel

Amos - Amos

Obad - Obadiah

Jonah - Jonah

Mic - Micah

Nah - Nahum

Hab - Habakkuk

Zeph - Zephaniah

Hag - Haggai

Zech - Zechariah

Mal - Malachi

New Testament

Mat – Matthew	1 Tim – I Timothy
Mark – Mark	2 Tim – II Timothy
Luke – Luke	Tit - Titus
John – John	Philem - Philemon
Acts – Acts	Heb - Hebrews
Rom – Romans	Jas - James
1 Cor – I Corinthians	1 Pet – I Peter
2 Cor – II Corinthians	2 Pet – II Peter
Gal – Galatians	1 John – I John
Eph – Ephesians	2 John – II John
Phil – Philippians	3 John – III John
Col – Colossians	Jude - Jude
1 Thes – I Thessalonians	Rev - Revelation
2 Thes – II Thessalonians	

The Foundation

I Corinthians 15:1-4 "Moreover, brethren, I declare unto you the gospel which I preached unto you, which also ye have received, and wherein ye stand; By which also ye are saved, if ye keep in memory what I preached unto you, unless ye have believed in vain. For I delivered unto you first of all that which I also received, how that Christ died for our sins according to the scriptures; And that He was buried, and that He rose again the third day according to the scriptures."

Romans 10:9-10 "That if thou shalt confess with thy mouth the Lord Jesus, and shalt believe in thine heart that God hath raised Him from the dead, thou shalt be saved. For with the heart man believeth unto righteousness; and with the mouth confession is made unto salvation."

John 3:16-17 "For God so loved the world, that He gave His only begotten Son, that whosoever believeth in Him should not perish, but have everlasting life. For God sent not His Son into the world to condemn the world; but that the world through Him might be saved."

Questions & Answers

SECTION ONE

1) What is Salvation?

Salvation is a restored relationship with God the Father through Jesus Christ the Son.

2) How does one come into Salvation?

One comes into salvation by believing in and accepting the death, burial, and resurrection of Jesus; confessing and repenting from one's sins; asking God's forgiveness for one's sins and receiving God's gift for one's self.

3) What does it mean to restore?

Restore – To give back to the owner something previously lost or taken; to reinstate to a former office, dignity, position, etc. (Merriam-Webster Dictionary)

Examples:

Ps 23:3 "He restoreth my soul…"

Ps 51:12 "Restore unto me the joy of thy salvation…"

Joel 2:25 "And I will restore to you the years that the locusts have eaten…"

4) Why does man need his relationship with God the Father restored? (Gen 1:26-27, Gen 3:8-10, Jas 4:4)

Jas 4:4 "Ye adulterers and adulteresses, know ye not that the friendship of the world is enmity with God? Whosoever therefore will be a friend of the world is the enemy of God."

Man needs his relationship with God the Father restored because one of the results of sin is that man lost his position or state of being ONE with God. This oneness can be termed Communion. God desires communion with man and there is a void in man that can only be filled by being in communion with God. This communion does not allow "friendship" with or love of the world because the two are opposed to each other. Man's communion with God is based upon man being one with God the Father.

5) How is one saved?

<u>Eph</u> *2:8-9 "For by grace are ye saved through faith; and that not of yourselves: it is the gift of God: Not of works, lest any man should boast."*

Man cannot save himself. Therefore, it is through the grace of God and man's trust in Who God Is that man can be saved. Salvation is a gift that is available to ALL who will receive it. Salvation is not of works because man can never do enough to earn it. Jesus the Christ paid the price for salvation for All that will embrace it.

Please note the three variations of the salvation question:

1 – What is salvation?

2 – How does one come into salvation?

3 – How is one saved?

6) What was the instruction given to Adam in the Garden of Eden? (<u>Gen</u> 2:16-17)

"And the Lord God commanded the man, saying, Of every tree of the garden thou mayest freely eat: But of the tree of the knowledge of good and evil, thou shalt not eat of it: for in the day that thou eatest thereof thou shalt surely die."

The instruction given to Adam in the Garden of Eden was that he could freely eat of every tree of the garden except for The Tree of the Knowledge of Good and Evil. This was Adam's only restriction.

7) What was the difference in how Eve responded to the temptation of the serpent (Satan) and how Adam responded? (Gen 3:6, 1 Tim 2:14)

1 Tim 2:14 "And Adam was not deceived, but the woman being deceived was in the transgression."

Eve's response was that of having been deceived into believing that there would be no consequences for eating of The Tree of the Knowledge of Good and Evil. Adam, on the other hand, knew he was going against God's instruction. There is a lot of theory as to why Adam disobeyed, but apart from all of that the outcome remains the same – Adam did not follow God's instruction. God expects man to walk in obedience to His instructions, for in the obedience the blessing comes forth.

8) Who committed the first act of disobedience toward God?

Lucifer committed the first act of disobedience toward God. Pride caused him to think that he could rise above/be greater than God Who created him.

Is 14:12-15

Ezek 28:12-19

Prov 16:18 "Pride goeth before destruction and an haughty spirit before a fall."

9) Why did God drive the man out of the Garden of Eden? (Gen 3:22-24)

Gen 3:23 "Therefore the Lord God sent him forth from the garden of Eden, to till the ground from whence he was taken. So He drove out the man..."

God drove the man out of the Garden of Eden so that man could not eat of The Tree of Life. If man had eaten of The Tree of Life in his sinful (disobedient) state, God would not have been able to redeem him, and man would remain separated from God for all eternity. This was the beginning of the manifestation of God's Plan of Salvation which was already in place before the foundation of the world.

10) What has Jesus saved the Christ follower from? (Memory tip: 3 P's)

Jesus has saved the Christ follower from:

The Penalty of Sin – Rom 6:21-23
"What fruit had ye then in those things whereof ye are now ashamed? For the end of those things is death. But now being made free from sin, and become servants to God, ye have your fruit unto holiness, and the end everlasting life. For the wages of sin is death: but the gift of God is eternal life through Jesus Christ our Lord."

The <u>Power</u> of Sin – <u>Rom</u> 6:11-14

"Likewise reckon ye also yourselves to be dead indeed unto sin, but alive unto God through Jesus Christ our Lord. Let not sin reign in your mortal body, that ye should obey it in the lusts thereof. Neither yield ye your members as instruments of unrighteousness unto sin: but yield yourselves unto God, as those that are alive from the dead, and your members as instruments of righteousness unto God. For sin shall not have dominion over you: for ye are not under the law, but under grace."

The <u>Presence</u> of Sin (future) – <u>Rev</u> 21:23-27

"And the twelve gates were twelve pearls; every several gate was of one pearl: and the street of the city was pure gold, as it were transparent glass. And I saw no temple therein: for the Lord God Almighty and the Lamb are the temple of it. And the city had no need of the sun, neither of the moon, to shine in it: for the glory of God did lighten it, and the Lamb is the light thereof. And the nations of them which are saved shall walk in the light of it: and the kings of the earth do bring their glory and honour into it. And

the gates of it shall not be shut at all by day: for there shall be no

night there. And they shall bring the glory and honour of the

nations into it. And there shall in no wise enter into it any thing

that defileth, neither whatsoever worketh abomination, or maketh a

lie: but they which are written in the Lamb's book of life."

11) What was Adam and Eve's attempt to remedy the predicament they got themselves into? (Gen 3:7-8)

Gen 3:7 *"And the eyes of them both were opened, and they knew that they were naked; and they sewed fig leaves together and made themselves aprons."*

Adam and Eve covered themselves with leaves. This is the first attempt of man trying to save himself by his own efforts. In other words, man was trying to save himself by works. God saves/God covers. Adam and Eve were attempting to hide the fact that they had lost their covering of the righteousness of God. God always sees through man's feeble efforts to cover up sin/disobedience. Man's efforts will never be enough!

12) What are the 3 areas of sin that the Christ follower must battle in his/her life? (<u>Gen</u> 3:6, <u>1 John</u> 2:16)

<u>1 John</u> 2:16 "For all that is in the world, the lust of the flesh, and the lust of the eyes, and the pride of life, is not of the Father, but is of the world."

The Lust of the Flesh, The Lust of the Eyes, The Pride of Life

- "The woman saw that the tree was good for food" – Lust of the Flesh.
- "That it was pleasant to the eyes" – Lust of the Eyes.
- "A tree desired to make one wise" – Pride of Life.

13) Who was the first to shed blood/kill in the Bible?

The Lord God was the first to shed blood/kill in the Bible.

Gen 3:21 "Unto Adam also and to his wife did the Lord God make coats of skins and clothed them."

This was the establishment of God setting in place that the blood of specific animal sacrifices be used to cover man's sins until the Perfect Sacrifice would come in and through Jesus Christ. Remember that God must ALWAYS cover. Man cannot cover himself when it comes to sin in his life. If man chooses to cover his own sin, he will eventually pay the ultimate price for it.

14) Why did Satan choose the serpent to work through? (Gen 3:1, Ezek 28:12-19, 2 Cor 11:14)

Gen 3:1 "Now the serpent was more subtil than any beast of the field which the Lord God had made. And he said unto the woman, Yea, hath God said, Ye shall not eat of every tree of the garden?"

31

Satan chose the serpent to work through because:

- *The serpent was: Subtil (subtle) – sly, cunning, clever, discerning.*
- *The serpent "lent" itself to Satan's influence/use.*
- *The serpent was a beautiful creature – not only physically, but in a way that it was able to hold Eve's attention in order to keep her engaged in conversation.*

15) What changes came about as a result of man's sin? (<u>Gen</u> 3:16-19)

"Unto the woman He said, I will greatly multiply thy sorrow and thy conception; in sorrow thou shalt bring forth children; and thy desire shall be to thy husband, and he shall rule over thee. And unto Adam He said, Because thou hast hearkened unto the voice of thy wife, and hast eaten of the tree, of which I commanded thee,

saying, Thou shalt not eat of it: cursed is the ground for thy sake;

in sorrow shalt thou eat of it all the days of thy life; Thorns also

and thistles shall it bring forth to thee; and thou shalt eat the herb

of the field; In the sweat of thy face shalt thou eat bread, till thou

return unto the ground; for out of it wast thou taken: for dust thou

art, and unto dust shalt thou return."

The changes that came about as a result of man's sin were:

- *Sorrow/pain during the woman's pregnancy and childbirth.*

- *The woman would be subject to her husband.*

- *The ground was cursed.*

- *Man would have to toil.*

- *Thorns and thistles came forth out of the ground.*

- *Man's communion/oneness with God was broken.*

- *Time as it is now known began.*

- *Man would be subject to sickness and disease.*

- *Man's body would grow old and deteriorate and eventually die.*

Man had additional responsibilities added to what the Lord God initially intended for him which are found in <u>Gen</u> 1:28 – "And God blessed them and God said unto them, Be fruitful and multiply and replenish the earth and subdue it; and have dominion over the fish of the sea and over the fowl of the air and over every living thing that moveth upon the earth."

16) Why wasn't Adam and Eve's solution for their disobedience appeasing to God?

Adam and Eve's solution for their disobedience was not appeasing to God because they took it upon themselves to cover themselves. Instead of coming before God, they hid themselves thinking that their sin would be hidden. They did what they thought was right in their own eyes. Man, still to this day tries to do the same, but the Lord God sees all. God in His omniscience already had a plan in place for man's disobedience. Man's solutions for his disobedience will always fall short.

17) Why wasn't Cain's offering acceptable to the Lord God? (Gen 4:1-5)

Gen 4:3-5 "And in process of time it came to pass, that Cain brought of the fruit of the ground an offering unto the Lord. And Abel, he also brought of the firstlings of his flock and of the fat thereof. And the Lord had respect unto Abel and to his offering: But unto Cain and to his offering He had not respect. And Cain was very wroth, and his countenance fell."

Cain's offering was not acceptable to the Lord because the offering that he brought was not according to God's instructions. The offering was supposed to be a Sin Offering which meant it had to be a blood sacrifice. Cain had been taught by his father Adam that sin offerings required blood sacrifice. Cain chose to do it his way and God gave him opportunity to make it right, but he instead chose to rebel.

Heb 9:22 "And almost all things are by the law purged with blood; and without shedding of blood is no remission (forgiveness)."

18) Is there a difference/significance between saying the blood of Jesus was "spilled" and the blood of Jesus was "shed/poured out?" Does it matter?

Yes, there is a difference and it does matter. Saying the blood of Jesus was spilled denotes that what Jesus experienced on behalf of man was an accident – no real significance behind it. Saying the blood of Jesus was shed or poured out denotes that there was a purpose. It was intentional. The purpose being the payment for man's sin so that man could be redeemed.

Something to Think About

Cain

The discussion concerning Cain's offering focuses on <u>Gen</u> 4:1-5. Looking a little further, one will find the Lord God speaking directly to Cain pertaining to his offering. The Lord God tells Cain that if he does well, he will be accepted and if he does not well, he will not be accepted.

So, what is this acceptance? This acceptance is following the instructions of the Lord God. The Lord God tells Cain that sin is lying at his door when he does not do well. This shows us more succinctly that the Lord God is dealing with Cain concerning his sin and that He is genuinely concerned about the sin in man's life. The Lord God desires that man be just as concerned. The Lord God wants man to do what is necessary to live free from sin and when sin does arise, He wants man to get right before Him.

Judgement

This word is used very loosely, and people tend to mix the World System **with and into** the Kingdom of God. This is where the confusion comes in and, since there is a lack of understanding, people (saved and unsaved) get offended and do not want to deal with issues at hand.

The purpose of judgement, as we see in our court system, is to pass or execute a sentence. It really does not deal with right or wrong. Just based upon the evidence presented a sentence is executed. This is also the judgement the Lord God will have – based upon what man did with the Breath of Life he was given – man will be sentenced to Eternal Life or Eternal Death.

The authority that the saints of God have to "judge" is not to execute a sentence, but to be **discerners of right and wrong, good and evil according to The Word of God.**

Lord grant me the wisdom to

Discern between good and evil,

Discern between right and wrong,

Discern between what's important and what's not

important,

That I may know how to judge righteously,

And know how to conduct myself in all situations.

Amen.

Quiz One

1) Why did God drive the man out of the garden?

2) What has Jesus saved those that trust in Him from?

3) How does one come into salvation?

4) What does it mean to restore?

5) How is one saved?

6) What are the 3 areas of sin that the believer must battle in his/her life?

7) What is salvation?

8) Why wasn't Cain's offering acceptable to the Lord?

SECTION TWO

19) What is man's penalty for sin? (Ezek 18:20, Rom 6:23)

Ezek 18:20 *"The soul that sinneth, it shall die. The son shall not bear the iniquity of the father, neither shall the father bear the iniquity of the son: the righteousness of the righteous shall be upon him, and the wickedness of the wicked shall be upon him."*

Man's penalty for sin is Death. This death is two-fold. There is a Spiritual Death and a Physical Death. Death came about as a result of man's sin in The Garden of Eden.

Spiritual Death – A break in the communion (oneness) between God and man.

Physical Death – Man's body ages, deteriorates, and is susceptible to sickness and disease.

20) Who paid the penalty for man's sin and when was it paid? (<u>Rom</u> 5:6-8, <u>Rev</u> 13:8)

<u>Rom</u> 5:6-8 *"For when we yet without strength, in due time Christ died for the ungodly. For scarcely for a righteous man will one die: yet peradventure for a good man some would even dare to die. But God commendeth His love toward us, in that, while we were yet sinners, Christ died for us."*

<u>Rev</u> 13:8 *"And all that dwell upon the earth shall worship Him, whose names are not written in the Book of Life of the Lamb slain from the foundation of the world."*

Jesus Christ paid the penalty for man's sin. He took the punishment and voluntarily laid down His life on behalf of man. The shedding of His blood made it possible for man to be forgiven and redeemed.

Jesus in the Spirit paid the price before the foundation of the world.
Man's redemption was already in the plan of God the Father.

21) Why does God hate sin? (<u>Lev</u> 20:26, <u>Is</u> 59:2)

<u>Lev</u> 20:26 "And ye shall be holy unto Me: for I the Lord am holy,
and have severed you from other people, that ye should be mine."

<u>Is</u> 59:2 "But your iniquities have separated between you and your
God, and your sins have hid His face from you, that He will not
hear."

*God hates sin because He is **HOLY**. Sin brings about/causes a*
separation between God and man. Sin cannot and will not be in
the presence of the Lord.

22) Why was Jesus qualified to pay the price for man's sin?

John 1:29 "...Behold the Lamb of God, which taketh away the sin of the world."

Jesus was qualified to pay the price for man's sin because He was conceived by the Holy Ghost. Therefore, man's sin nature did not pass onto Him – _Mat_ 1:18, _Luke_ 1:26-35.

John the Baptist declared Jesus to be The Lamb of God – _John_ 1:29, 36.

Jesus never sinned – _2 Cor_ 5:21, _Heb_ 4:15.

Jesus came to seek and to save the lost – _Luke_ 19:10.

Man can only get to God the Father through Jesus Christ the Son – _John_ 14:6.

23) What is the difference in how Adam was formed and in how Eve was made? What is the main significance of this difference? (Gen 2:7, Gen 2:18, 21-22)

Gen 2:7 "And the Lord God formed man of the dust of the ground and breathed into his nostrils the breath of life; and man became a living soul."

Gen 2:18, 21-22 "And the Lord God said, It is not good that the man should be alone; I will make him an help meet for him. And the Lord God caused a deep sleep to fall upon Adam, and he slept: and He took one his ribs, and closed up the flesh instead thereof; And the rib, which the Lord God had taken from man, made He a woman, and brought her unto the man."

The difference in how Adam was formed and in how Eve was made is:

God formed Adam from the dust of the ground. Adam was the first of God's creation in which God was "physically" involved. All other of God's creation was spoken into existence. God was intimately involved in the creation of Adam.

God made Eve from one of Adam's ribs. Based upon what God put into Adam, He made Eve "fit" for him. The scripture says "an help meet for him." Eve was designed to help Adam meet the responsibilities that God had given him.

The main significance between the creations of Adam and Eve is that Adam was formed from the dust of the earth and Eve was made from the flesh of Adam. The flesh represents the "weak" part of mankind. The flesh must be watched over, kept under subjection, and protected. Otherwise, it gets into and causes trouble. In similar fashion, a husband is to watch over and protect his wife. This is where Adam failed in The Garden of Eden when Eve was engaged in conversation with the serpent.

Rom 7:18 *"For I know that in me (that is, in my flesh) dwelleth no good thing: for to will is present with me, but to perform that which is good I find not."*

24) What is the similarity between Enoch and Noah and what does it mean? (Gen 5:24, Gen 6:9)

Gen 5:24 *"And Enoch walked with God: and he was not; for God took him."*

Gen 6:9 *"These are the generations of Noah: Noah was a just man and perfect in his generations, and Noah walked with God."*

The similarity between Enoch and Noah is that the scripture says Enoch and Noah WALKED WITH God. This means that they were obedient to His Word and that they trusted in Him. Even though mankind was disobedient and sinful, Enoch and Noah strived to be pleasing in the sight of God and lived their lives accordingly. This does not mean that they did not sin, but that they handled their sin according to the instructions given by God.

25) Why did God decide to destroy the earth He created? (<u>Gen</u> 6:1-7)

<u>Gen</u> *6:5 "And God saw that the wickedness of man was great in the earth and that every imagination of the thoughts of his heart was only evil continually."*

Evil was running rampant through the earth and everything about man was evil. Man was corrupt and totally evil. The earth needed to be cleansed. As we use water daily to wash and cleanse, God used water to "wash and cleanse" the earth from the evil that had contaminated it. God still loved man, but man had crossed the point of no return in his sin.

26) How long did it take Noah to build the ark? (<u>Gen</u> 6:1-7)

Gen 6:3 "And the Lord said, My Spirit shall not always strive with man, for that he also is flesh: yet his days shall be an hundred and twenty years."

Noah was allotted 120 years to build the ark. Man's time for repentance was set at 120 years and within this time frame Noah's task was to build the ark.

27) Who was the oldest man to have ever lived? (_Gen_ 5:1-32)

Gen 5:27 "And all the days of Methuselah were nine hundred sixty and nine years: and he died."

The oldest man to have ever lived was Methuselah, 969 years.

28) Who were these "sons of God?" (_Gen_ 6:1-4)

Gen 6:1-2 *"And it came to pass, when men began to multiply on the face of the earth, and daughters were born unto them, That the sons of God saw the daughters of men that they were fair; and they took them wives of all which they chose."*

These "sons of God" were the men who, at that time, trusted in the Lord and were obedient to His Word. The "daughters of men" that the scripture refers to were the women who, at that time, did not walk in the ways of the Lord.

Some would say these "sons of God" were angels, but nowhere in the Word of God is it supported that angels (good or evil) can have or have had physical relations with mankind. This is another example of deception that has been purported down through the years and it has misled the people of God.

29) What caused or what was the reason for such corruption upon the earth at that time?

Man had an inherent sin nature resultant from the disobedience of Adam. So, this is not the issue. The issue is that the "sons of God" intermingled with and married the "daughters of men." The result of these relations was that the hearts of the sons of God were turned away from God the Father and the children that were born out of these relationships were not brought up and taught in the ways of the Lord. This turning away brought about great wickedness upon the earth and every imagination of the thoughts of men's hearts was only evil continually.

God later warns and stresses throughout scripture that His people be separate from the ways of the world and to not be "unequally yoked." "Be ye holy, for I Am Holy" (2 Cor 6:14, 1 Pet 1:16).

30) Why did God "instruct" Noah in how to build the ark as opposed to allowing Noah to build it on his own? (Gen 6:14-16)

"Make thee an ark of gopher wood; rooms shalt thou make in the ark, and shalt pitch it within and without with pitch. And this is the fashion which thou shalt make it of: The length of the ark shall be three hundred cubits, the breadth of it fifty cubits, and the height of it thirty cubits. A window shalt thou make to the ark, and in a cubit shalt thou finish it above; and the door of the ark shalt thou set in the side thereof; with lower, second, and third stories shalt thou make it.

God instructed Noah because He knew what would be required of the ark for it to house and sustain the life that it would hold. It had to be big enough for all the occupants, it had to be structurally sound, and it had to be watertight. God kept Noah from adding any of his own ideas or imagination.

31) Since Noah was the one who found "grace" in the eyes of God, why was his family allowed to come with him into the ark?

Noah's family was allowed to come into the ark because they would bear the responsibility of starting to repopulate the earth. God is "choosing" to use Noah and his family for this endeavor. God could have easily made another woman for Noah to fulfill this purpose. Therefore, the greater reason that Noah's family was allowed to come into the ark is that Noah was The Covering for his family. Since Noah "walked" with God, he sanctified his family. The scripture does not mention the relational dynamics between God and the members of Noah's family, but because of Noah's faith his family was covered. Therefore, it is so important that the husband and father be in right relation with God the Father. He bears a lot of responsibility for his family.

32) What is the significance in how the ark was closed? (Gen 7:16)

"And they that went in, went in male and female of all flesh, as God commanded him: and the Lord shut him in."

The significance in how the ark was closed is that God closed/shut the ark. Neither Noah nor anyone else could open it. When God says that the allotted time has come to a close or end, man can do nothing about it.

Noah certainly would have opened the door of the ark to let people in when the water started to rise, but God made it so that he could not. This does not mean that the Lord God no longer loved the ones that were left on the outside. He gave them opportunity, 120 years, and they failed to take advantage of it. God does not and will not compromise His Word. This also signifies that when God closes the door of salvation it cannot be reopened by man.

33) How were the animals chosen that were to be brought into the ark? (Gen 7:2-3)

"Of every clean beast thou shalt take to thee by sevens, the male and his female: and of beasts that are not clean by two, the male

and his female. Of fowls also of the air by sevens, the male and the

female; to keep seed alive upon the face of all the earth."

It has often been heard that the animals were brought in one male

and one female of each kind. What does the Word of God say?

7 male and 7 females of the clean

2 male and 2 females of the unclean

34) How big was the ark? What were the measurements of
it? (Gen 6:15)

"And this is the fashion which thou shalt make it of: The length of

the ark shall be three hundred cubits, the breadth of it fifty cubits,

and the height of it thirty cubits."

According to the Word of God, the ark was:

300 cubits long x 50 cubits wide x 30 cubits high

300cu (18in / 1cu) (1ft / 12in) = 450 ft long

50cu (18in / 1cu) (1ft / 12in) = 75 ft wide

30cu (18in / 1cu) (1ft / 12in) = 45 ft high

450ft (1yd / 3ft) = 150 yds

1 ½ FOOTBAL FIELDS LONG!!

35) Looking at the big picture, what did the ark of Noah represent and what is the message for today?

The ark represented Salvation. The ark represented Jesus Christ. Noah trusted in the Lord and because of his trust he and his family were saved by way of the ark while the world was condemned.

*The message for today is that God desires **ALL** to be saved (2 Pet 3:9), but He has a set time period for man to come into salvation. When the door closes, time is up.*

"The Lord is not slack concerning His promise, as some men count slackness; but is longsuffering to us-ward, not willing that any should perish, but that all should come to repentance."

36) What was the resting place for the ark of Noah and what did it symbolize? (<u>Gen</u> 8:4, 20-22)

<u>Gen</u> *8:4, 20 "And the ark rested in the seventh month, on the seventeenth day of the month, upon the mountains of Ararat. And Noah builded an altar unto the Lord; and took of every clean beast, and of every clean fowl, and offered burnt-offerings on the altar."*

The resting place for the ark of Noah was the mountains of Ararat. Ararat represented New Beginning and Holy Ground. The earth had been washed and cleansed by the Word of God – God SAID that He would bring a flood of waters upon the earth. As Noah, his family, and the animals departed from the ark they would be the ones to replenish the earth (New Beginning) and Noah offered worship and sacrifice upon the mountain to the Lord God (Holy Ground).

37) Why was God displeased with man's ingenuity? (<u>Gen</u> 11:1-9)

<u>Gen</u> *11:4-6 "And they said, Go to, let us build us a city and a tower, whose top may reach unto heaven; and let us make us a name, lest we be scattered abroad upon the face of the whole earth. And the Lord came down to see the city and the tower, which the children of men builded. And the Lord said, Behold, the people is one, and they have all one language; and this they begin to do: and now nothing will be restrained from them, which they have imagined to do."*

God was displeased with man's ingenuity because man was again doing that which was right in his own eyes (remember Cain). He did not consult God in building a tower to heaven and God did not instruct him to do so. This is also an example of man trying to get to God on his own terms and by his own efforts. Although this is

an event which occurred in the Old Testament, it is a prelude to

the declaration made by Jesus in the New Testament – John 14:6 "I

Am the Way, the Truth, and the Life: no man cometh unto the

Father, but by Me."

38) What was the significance in God's instructions to Abram to leave all that he knew? (Gen 12:1-3)

Gen 12:1 "Now the Lord had said unto Abram, Get thee out of thy

country, and from thy kindred, and from thy father's house, unto a

land that I will shew thee."

The significance in God's instructions to Abram to leave all that he

knew was that God wanted to get Abram to a place where he could

fully trust the Lord God. God had to get Abram away from that

which was familiar and convenient and that which could influence

or deter him from God's plan and purpose.

God will also do that in the lives of those that have put their trust in Him as well. So that His Plan and Purpose can be fulfilled, God will remove people, places, and things from the lives of His people in order to bring them to a place of total trust and submission.

39) How did man come about to speak the Word of God? (2 Pet 1:21)

"For the prophecy came not in old time by the will of man: but holy men of God spake as they were moved by the Holy Ghost."

Man came about to speak the Word of God under God's direction. Holy men of God were moved (inspired) by the Holy Ghost to speak the Word of God. Take note that the scripture says, "Holy men of God." These were men who had been set apart and sanctified by the Lord God. These were men to whom God could entrust His Word.

40) What must take place in a person's life for him/her to understand the Word of God? (1 Cor 2:14-16)

"But the natural man receiveth not the things of the Spirit of God: for they are foolishness unto him: neither can he know them, because they are spiritually discerned. But he that is spiritual judgeth all things, yet he himself is judged of no man. For who hath known the mind of the Lord, that he may instruct him? But we have the mind of Christ."

In order to understand the Word of God, a person must come into SALVATION – BE BORN AGAIN. The natural or carnal mind attempts to "explain" the Word of God but will always come up lacking. The spiritual mind is open to the revelation of the Word of God by the Holy Spirit.

John 16:13 "Howbeit when He, the Spirit of truth, is come, He will guide you into all truth: for He shall not speak of Himself; but whatsoever He shall hear, that shall He speak: and He will shew

you things to come."

41) What does <u>Timothy</u> say about the Word of God? (<u>2 Tim</u> 3:16-17)

"All scripture is given by inspiration of God, and is profitable for doctrine, for reproof, for correction, for instruction in righteousness: That the man of God may be perfect, thoroughly furnished unto all good works."

All scripture is given by inspiration of God – The authors were moved or driven to perform their writings.

Profitable for doctrine – Teachings and instructions that are beneficial which should be believed in and adhered to.

For reproof – Makes known what is wrong or out of the way.

For correction – Makes known what should be done.

For instruction in righteousness – Guidance in how to be in right standing with God.

42) Why is the written Word of God such a unique book? (Heb 4:12)

"For the Word of God is quick, and powerful, and sharper than any twoedged sword, piercing even to the dividing asunder of soul and spirit, and of the joints and marrow, and is a discerner of the thoughts and intents of the heart."

The written Word of God is such a unique book because in reading it a person's life can be transformed. The written Word of God is A BOOK OF LIFE. It can reach the darkest places of a person's innermost being and cut out that which is tainted. God then heals that wound and puts Himself in the place of that which was removed. That which a person can hide and keep secret from others, when the Word of God is read and heard the hidden and secret will be exposed.

43) What is the instruction given to the believer and why is it so important? (2 Tim 2:15)

"Study to shew thyself approved unto God, a workman that needeth not to be ashamed, rightly dividing the word of truth."

The instruction given to the believer is to study the Word of God. In studying the Word of God, the believer's life and way of thinking can be transformed. This is so important because this puts the believer in a position to stand before God in the righteousness of Jesus Christ so that the life he or she lives now is pleasing to God and according to His Word.

44) What role does Grace play in salvation and why is it so important? (Eph 2:8-9)

"For by grace are ye saved through faith; and that not of yourselves: it is the gift of God: Not of works, lest any man should boast."

Grace – The power of God to do for us that which we cannot do for ourselves.

God uses His Grace to save a person. A person cannot save him or herself, so God allows His grace to bridge the gap. It is so important because without God's grace no one can be saved. God in and through Jesus Christ took man's sin and paid what was required for it. This was and is something man cannot do and still stand in the presence of God.

45) What is religion according to man's perspective?

Religion according to man's perspective is "the belief in a god or group of gods; an organized system of beliefs, ceremonies, and rules used to worship a god or group of gods" (Merriam-Webster

Dictionary). It is man using his own efforts to get to God. It is

man offering to God what he thinks God will be pleased with.

Although there is an aura of "godliness," when it is examined

closely the flaws and errors are exposed because it is based upon

man's efforts, his works, what he thinks is right, and not what God

has spoken and set forth. Also, and most importantly, there is no

true, authentic, and lasting remedy for sin.

46) What is religion according to the Word of God? (Jas 1:27)

"Pure religion and undefiled before God and the Father is this, To

visit the fatherless and widows in their affliction, and to keep

himself unspotted from the world."

Religion according to the Word of God is "to visit the fatherless

and widows in their affliction and to keep one's self unspotted from

the world."

Taking care of the orphans and widows and not being

contaminated by the world system is God's perspective of "pure religion." God desires to have a RELATIONSHIP with man, not

ceremonies and ordinances. Therefore, He never mentions religion

as man sees it. God has set forth A WAY OF LIFE for those that

trust Him through Jesus Christ.

<u>*Mic*</u> *6:8 "He hath shewed thee, O man, what is good; and what*

doth the Lord require of thee, but to do justly, and to love mercy,

and to walk humbly with thy God."

<u>*Eccl*</u> *12:13 "Let us hear the conclusion of the whole matter: Fear*

God and keep His commandments: for this is the whole duty of

man."

47) What is the prevailing theme that runs through the Book
of Judges?

The prevailing theme that runs through the Book of Judges is, "In

those days there was no king in Israel, every man did that which

was right in his own eyes" (<u>*Judg*</u> *17:6, 21:25).*

Quiz Two

Fill in the blanks.

1)   For _____ world that He _____

_____

_____ whosoever

believeth in Him _____

but _____

_____ .

2) _____ is death _____

_____ is _____

_____ .

3) I set _____ and death __

_____ .

4) In those days _____ every man __

_____ which _____

_____.

5) _____ the _____ the _____

_____ and the _____. No man _____

_____ but _____.

6) There is a way _____ man,

but the end _____ are the _____

_____.

7) _____ pursueth _____.

Word Bank

sinners   which seemeth right unto a   Life

before you life   God so loved the

for the wages of sin   there was no king in Israel   thereof

I Am   did that

gave His only begotten Son that   choose life   Way

should not perish

but the gift of God   evil   Truth   ways of death

have everlasting life

was right in his own eyes   cometh unto the Father

eternal life through Jesus Christ our Lord

through Me

SECTION THREE

48) How did David come to be in the situation in which he found himself in 2 Sam 11?

2 Sam 11:1 *"And it came to pass, after the year was expired, at the time when kings go forth to battle, that David sent Joab, and his servants with him, and all Israel; and they destroyed the children of Ammon , and besieged Rabbah. But David tarried still at Jerusalem."*

David came to be in this situation because he chose to stay home when he should have been with his men leading them in battle. He was not where he was supposed to be – he was not in his PLACE.

When the Christ follower is not in his/her "place" it opens the door for the enemy's influence and gives the flesh opportunity to rise up and lead one into sin.

49) What is Mercy?

Mercy is the time God gives man after he has walked in disobedience (sinned) to come before Him in confession and repentance. Lam 3:22 says, "It is of the Lord's mercies that we are not consumed because His compassions fail not." God is not sitting and waiting to come down on man, but sin demands judgement. Therefore, because of His Mercy, we have time to come before the Lord before He responds according to His Word.

50) How did mercy work in David's life in Ps 51?

Ps 51:1-3 "Have mercy upon me, O God, according to thy lovingkindness: according unto the multitude of thy tender mercies blot out my transgressions. Wash me thoroughly from mine iniquity, and cleanse me from my sin. For I acknowledge my transgressions: and my sin is ever before me."

David was guilty of murder and according to the Word of God he should have been put to death. In Ps 51 David gives a full-blown confession of his sin. He asks God to wash and cleanse him and to restore their broken relationship. Because of David's confession and repentance, the death sentence was stayed, but he had to deal with the consequences of his sin the rest of his life.

For other reference, see Gen 9:6 (Law of First Mention), Lev 24:17, Num 35:30-31, 2 Sam 12:1-15.

Gen 9:6 "Whoso sheddeth man's blood, by man shall his blood be shed: for in the image God made He man."

51) What consequences did David experience as a result of his sin?

The consequences David experienced as a result of his sin were:

Death of first-born child.

Privilege and honor of building Temple taken away.

Family turmoil.

Son raped daughter.

Son killed brother.

Son attempted to kill David.

52) What is reconciliation? (Rom 5:10, 2 Cor 5:18)

Rom 5:10 "For if, when we were enemies, we were reconciled to God by the death of His Son, much more, being reconciled, we shall be saved by His life."

Reconciliation is "the act of causing two people or groups to become friendly again after an argument or disagreement" (Merriam-Webster Dictionary).

Reconciliation between God and man is their relationship being brought back into balance.

53) How does God use grace in the life of the saint when he/she is challenged with sin?

Reference the definition for grace – the power of God to do for us that which we cannot do for ourselves. When challenged with sin, the saint now has the power of God through the Holy Spirit to say no to it. The Christ follower does not have to give in to the temptation and then allow sin to run its course. Also, as <u>Rom</u> 6:1 states, believers do not continue in sin in an attempt to get more grace. This is backwards thinking. Sin has consequences. Believers are dead to sin, and their desire should be to live free from it.

<u>Rom</u> 6:1-2 "What shall we say then? Shall we continue in sin, that grace may abound? God forbid. How shall we that are dead to sin, live any longer therein?"

54) How should the saint of God view him/herself when it comes to sin and what should be the conduct of that saint?

The saint of God should see him or herself dead to sin. Sin should not reign in his or her body and there should be obedience to the Lord and not the lust of the flesh. The Christ follower's entire being should be yielded to the Lord for righteousness.

Rom 6:11-13 "Likewise reckon ye also yourselves to be dead indeed unto sin, but alive unto God through Jesus Christ our Lord. Let not sin reign in your mortal body, that ye should obey it in the lusts thereof. Neither yield ye your members as instruments of unrighteousness unto sin: but yield yourselves unto God, as those that are alive from the dead, and your members as instruments of righteousness unto God."

55) How is the believer buried with Jesus Christ?

The believer is buried with Jesus Christ through Baptism. Jesus bore the believer's sins in His body on the cross, died, and was buried. The believer's physical baptism in water is his/her outward expression that the believer has embraced what Jesus has done for him/her and that the believer has died to sin and is burying it – the old man.

Rom 6:4 "Therefore we are buried with Him by baptism into death: that like as Christ was raised up from the dead by the glory of the Father, even so we also should walk in newness of life."

56) What is the significance in Jude using the phrase "common salvation" and what are the saints of God to do concerning it? (Jude)

Jude 3 "Beloved, when I gave all diligence to write unto you of the common salvation, it was needful for me write unto you, and exhort you that ye should earnestly contend for the faith which was once delivered unto the saints."

Jude is emphasizing that the salvation he is referring to is the same salvation that the saints before him preached, taught, and wrote about. Nothing has changed. Salvation is still in and through Jesus Christ. Because of the prevailing apostasy at that time, Jude found it needful to remind his audience of this.

Jude also found it needful to exhort the believers to contend for the faith. In other words, Jude was telling the Christ followers that they needed to fight for the faith (their faith) in Jesus Christ. There were some that had found a way in and they were teaching heresies. The believers of this present day are faced with the same task – they must fight for The Truth of the Word of God.

57) What does Jude mean when he says, "the way of Cain?"

<u>Jude</u> 11 *"Woe unto them! For they have gone in the way of Cain and ran greedily after the error of Balaam for reward and perished in the gainsaying of Core."*

When Jude says, "the way of Cain" he is making reference to doing something "your way" and not the way that has been instructed by the Lord God.

58) What are the two (2) unique characteristics of <u>Psalm</u> 119?

The two (2) unique characteristics of <u>Ps</u> 119 are:

1 - <u>Ps</u> 119 is the longest single section of scripture (176 verses).

2 - Each verse of <u>Ps</u> 119 references the Word of God.

59) What is the command given by Jesus? (<u>John</u> 3:3-8)

<u>John</u> 3:7 "Marvel not that I said unto thee, Ye must be born again."

The command given by Jesus is "ye must be born again." Man

cannot see or enter the Kingdom of God unless there is a new birth

(regeneration – man dies to self and becomes alive to God through

faith in Jesus Christ).

60) What is the promise given to man? (John 3:14-16)

John 3:16 "For God so loved the world, that He gave His only

begotten Son, that whosoever believeth in Him should not perish,

but have everlasting life."

The promise given to man is Eternal Life – "whosoever believeth in

Him should not perish but have everlasting life."

61) What choices does man have? (1 John 5:9-13, Deut 30:19)

1 John 5:10 "He that believeth on the Son of God hath the witness

in himself: he that believeth not God hath made Him a liar; because

he believeth not the record that God gave of His Son."

Man has two (2) choices from which to decide – he can either choose to believe in the Son of God or choose not to believe in the Son of God. There is no middle ground.

62) To what is man a servant to if he practices it? (John 8:34)

"Jesus answered them, Verily, verily, I say unto you, Whosoever committeth sin is the servant of sin."

Man is a servant to sin if he <u>practices</u> *sin. Man will inevitably commit sin because he still resides in a body of flesh. Thanks be to God that He extends to man His grace and mercy and that believers "have an advocate with the Father, Jesus Christ the Righteous."*

<u>1 John</u> 2:1 *"My little children, these things write I unto you, that ye sin not. And if any man sin, we have an advocate with the Father, Jesus Christ the righteous."*

1 John 1:9 "If we confess our sins, He is faithful and just to forgive us our sins, and to cleanse us from all unrighteousness."

63) What is the result of sin? (Jas 1:15)

"Then when lust hath conceived, it bringeth forth sin: and sin, when it is finished, bringeth forth death."

Sin brings about death! When the believer envisions or imagines (when lust hath conceived) that which is against God (all unrighteousness) sin is the outcome and when that sin has run its course it brings about death. No, the believer does not physically die, but his/her communion with the Lord God is broken and fellowship with the brothers and sisters in Christ is disrupted.

Note that James is not dealing with Salvation as Paul was in Rom 3:23.

"For all have sinned and come short of the glory of God."

64) What are the 3 creative acts of God? (Gen 1-2)

The 3 creative acts of God are:

1 – God spoke the light, the firmament, the vegetation, the herb, the fruit tree, the sun, the moon, the stars, the moving creature (water), the fowl, and the living creature (land) into existence.
Gen 1:1-25

2 – God formed man of the dust of the ground.
Gen 2:7 "And the Lord God formed man of the dust of the ground and breathed into his nostrils the breath of life; and man became a living soul."

3 – God made woman from man's rib.
Gen 2:18, 21-22 "And the Lord God said, It is not good that the man should be alone; I will make him an help meet for him. And the Lord God caused a deep sleep to fall upon Adam, and he slept: and He took one his ribs, and closed up the flesh instead thereof;

And the rib, which the Lord God had taken from man, made He a woman, and brought her unto the man."

65) What does <u>Gen</u> 1:26 reveal about Who God Is?

"And God said, Let us make man in our image, after our likeness…"

<u>Gen</u> 1:26 first reveals that God is a unique being. Secondly, that God somehow in some way is not a single solitary being or that He is multidimensional. In other words, there is more to God than one can know currently. To this point in scripture, God has not revealed much about Who He Is, but has revealed some of what He Can Do.

66) What does <u>Gen</u> 1:28 reveal about the earth?

"And God blessed them, and God said unto them, Be fruitful, and multiply, and replenish the earth, and subdue it: and have dominion over the fish of the sea, and over the fowl of the air, and over every living thing that moveth upon the earth."

Earth had a history before God's and man's introduction in the scripture. Man is (we are) not privy to that history, but we see God instructing the man (male and female) to be fruitful and multiply so that the earth can be replenished (filled or built up again). Also, God is instructing the man to get control of the earth (subdue it). So, it bears to reason that something happened between Gen 1:1 and Gen 1:2, but it is not revealed at this time.

Deut 29:29 "The secret things belong unto the Lord our God: but those things which are revealed belong unto us and to our children forever, that we may do all the words of this law."

Jer 4:23-26 "I beheld the earth, and, lo, it was without form, and void; and the heavens, and they had no light. I beheld the

89

mountains, and, lo, they trembled, and all the hills moved lightly. I beheld, and, lo, there was no man, and all the birds of the heavens were fled. I beheld, and, lo, the fruitful place was a wilderness, and all the cities thereof were broken down at the presence of the Lord, and by His fierce anger."

Notes

Quiz One Answers

1) Why did God drive the man out of the garden?

God drove the man out of the garden to keep him from eating of the fruit of The Tree of Life. If man had eaten from The Tree of Life in his sinful state, God would not have been able to redeem him and there would be no salvation for mankind.

2) What has Jesus saved those that trust in Him from?

The Penalty of Sin, The Power of Sin, The Presence of Sin (future)

3) How does one come into salvation?

One comes into salvation by believing in and accepting the death, burial, and resurrection of Jesus; confessing and repenting from one's sins; asking God's forgiveness for one's sins; receiving God's

gift for one's self.

4) What does it mean to restore?

To restore means to give back to the owner something previously

lost or taken; To reinstate to a former position, office, dignity, etc.

5) How is one saved?

One is saved by Grace through Faith – not of Works.

6) What are the 3 areas of sin that the believer must battle in his/her life?

The Lust of the Flesh, The Lust of the Eyes, The Pride of Life

7) What is salvation?

Salvation is a restored relationship with God the Father through Jesus Christ the Son.

8) Why wasn't Cain's offering acceptable to the Lord?

Cain's offering was supposed to be a sin offering. Cain's offering was not acceptable to the Lord because it was not according to God's instructions. Cain had been taught by his father Adam that the offering was to be a blood sacrifice. Cain chose to do it his way. He had opportunity to make it right, but instead chose to rebel.

Quiz Two Answers

Fill in the blanks.

1) For _God so loved the_ world that He _gave His only begotten son_ _that_ whosoever believeth in Him _should not perish_ but _have everlasting life_. _John_ 3:16

2) _For the wages of sin_ is death _but the gift of God_ is _eternal life through Jesus Christ our Lord_. _Rom_ 6:23

3) I set _before you life_ and death _choose life_. _Deut_ 30:19

4) In those days _there was no king in Israel_ every man _did that_ which _was right in his own eyes_. _Judg_ 21:25

5) *I Am* the *Way* the *Truth* and the *Life*. No man *cometh unto the Father* but *through Me*. *John* 14:6

6) There is a way *which seemeth right unto a* man, but the end *thereof* are the *ways of death*. *Prov* 14:12

7) *Evil* pursueth *sinners*. *Prov* 13:21

sinners   which seemeth right unto a   Life

before you life   God so loved the

for the wages of sin   there was no king in Israel   thereof

I Am   did that

gave His only begotten Son that   choose life   Way

should not perish

but the gift of God   evil   Truth   ways of death

have everlasting life

was right in his own eyes   cometh unto the Father

eternal life through Jesus Christ our Lord

through Me

Conclusion

As I close this work, I want to leave you with the following –
I trust that the questions, the answers, and the thought
provokers have inspired you in some way to want to know
the Lord God better and to grow closer to Him. I thank the
Lord God, His Son the Lord Jesus Christ, and the Holy Spirit
for inspiring me to go forth in this endeavor. I am just one
who desires to be a fit vessel for the Lord's use, and I
encourage you to desire the same.

To the one who is looking and searching for "a way" - Jesus
Christ is THE WAY!

To the Christ follower, entreat the Lord God on behalf of the
Body of Christ to open our eyes of understanding to
GREATER REVELATION. Not new revelation, but greater

revelation. The Lord God is not giving out any new revelations for He has already spoken in His Word. We just need our eyes opened to see it.

To God Be The Glory,

Karl W Law

John 1:1 – Jesus Christ **IS** God.

John 14:6 – Jesus Christ is the Way to God, the Truth of God, and True Life is in Him. The only way to get to God the Father is through Jesus Christ.

Acts 4:12 – Jesus is the only provision (name) given by God that ALL mankind may come into salvation.

Rom 3:23 – Paul was making a point to the Jews that there is no difference between them and the Gentiles when standing before the righteousness of God. The bigger picture being that all mankind is guilty of sin in the eyes of the Holy God.

Rom 6:23 – Mankind's just due for sin (emanating from an inherent sinful nature) is death (spiritual and physical), but because of God's awesome grace mankind can receive the gift of eternal life through Jesus Christ.

Rom 5:8 – God did not wait for mankind to "get right" because He knew it could never and would never happen. Therefore, because of His love, God implemented His plan of salvation through Jesus Christ even though man was still lost in sin.

1 Pet 2:24 – Jesus bore the believer's sins in His body and when He was nailed to the cross the believer's sins were nailed to that cross as well. As believers trust in the saving grace of Jesus, believers become dead to sin and live in the righteousness of Jesus. Believers are healed spiritually through that which He took on their behalf.

Rom 10:9 – As man completely embraces what Jesus has done for him (confessing with his mouth and believing in his heart or mind), he is submitting his total being in an act of faith to the finished work of Jesus and thereby he receives the gift of salvation.

<u>John</u> 1:12 – By believing who Jesus said He is opened the way for man to come into salvation (man had the power to come out of darkness) and become a child of God. This power even extended and extends to those who never met Jesus face to face but have the faith to believe in the authority that He has (that which He has spoken and that which has been spoken of Him).

*All scripture quotations are from the Holy Bible, King James Version, in the public domain.

Appendix

Question Topics and Corresponding Question Numbers

Salvation – Grace – Mercy

1, 2, 5, 10, 18, 31, 32, 35, 40, 44, 49, 50, 53, 56, 59, 60

The Book of Genesis

6, 7, 9, 11, 13, 14, 15, 16, 17, 23, 24, 26, 27, 28, 29, 30, 33, 34, 37,

38, 64, 65, 66

The Word of God

39, 41, 42, 43, 58

Religion

45, 46

The Book of Judges

47

Restoration – Reconciliation

3, 4, 52

Sin

8, 12, 19, 20, 21, 22, 25, 48, 51, 54, 57, 61, 62, 63

Baptism

55

New Beginning – Holy Ground

36

Glossary

- Faith – Trusting in the Lord Who Is God.

- Faith - Based upon Who God Is and His Word; we not only "believe in" God, we more so "believe" God.

- Grace – The power of God to do for man that which man cannot do for himself.

- True Worship – The submission of one's self in love to God's almighty authority.

- Trust – Committing one's self and wellbeing into the hands and care of the Lord.

- Trust – Complete abandonment to God.

About the Author

A skilled tradesman by profession, Karl is well known for his gift of repairing and maintaining motorized vehicles and machinery. Shortly after accepting Jesus Christ as his personal Lord and Savior in 1984, his special gift of repairing machinery would be used for repairing and leading lost souls to Jesus Christ. Karl answered the call and is now a licensed, ordained minister of God. Through his life and this book, Karl desires to enlighten and cultivate others in God's Word.

"My people are destroyed for lack of knowledge..."
Hosea 4:6

Karl truly has a heart for God's people; he desires to impart hope and knowledge of the Word in them through Jesus Christ. Karl resides in Detroit, Michigan with his wife and two daughters, and serves as associate minister at International Miracle Gospel Tabernacle Church.

For additional information or to request an author appearance, contact Karl at karlwlaw@gmail.com

www.ingramcontent.com/pod-product-compliance
Lightning Source LLC
Chambersburg PA
CBHW021836020426
42334CB00014B/655